All you need to create a world is some crayons. Hare and Bear have a whole box of colored crayons and lots of ideas. In this book they show you how to draw an airplane. If you watch how Hare and Bear do it, you can draw one too. Just copy the shapes from the colored box at the top of each page onto your own drawing. And soon you'll be flying!

Hare and Bear
Draw An Airplane

Diann Timms

Reader's Digest Kids
Pleasantville, N.Y.—Montreal

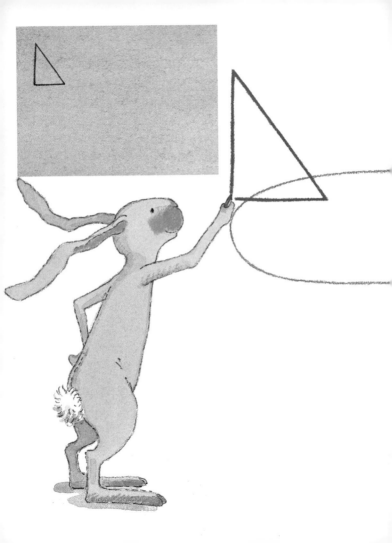

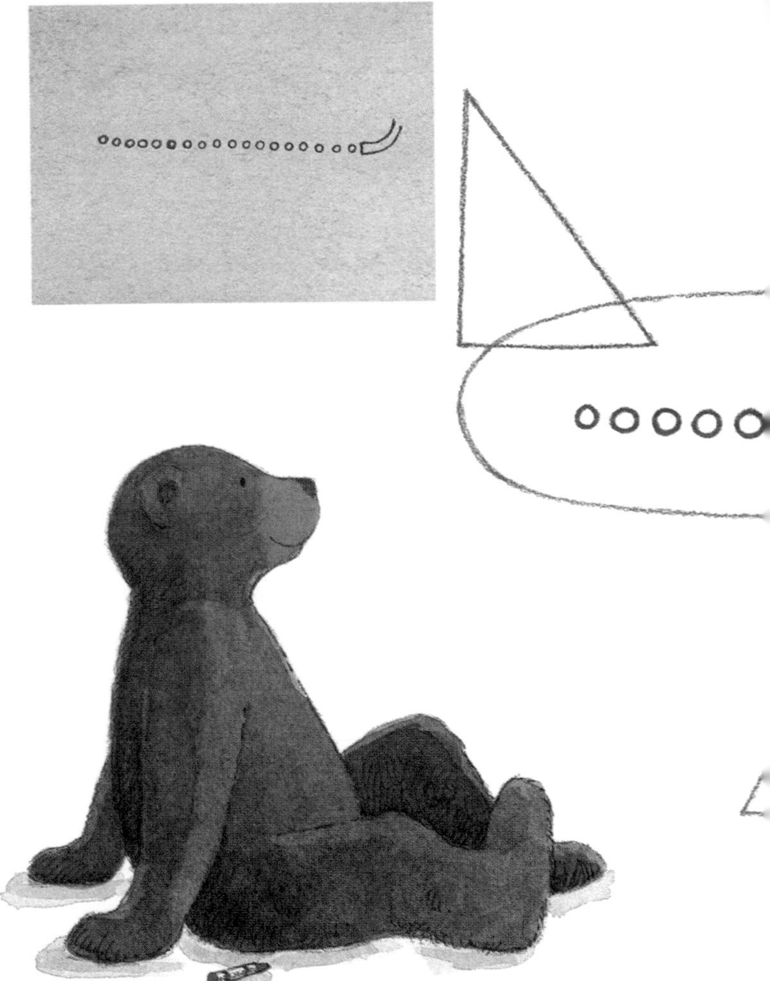

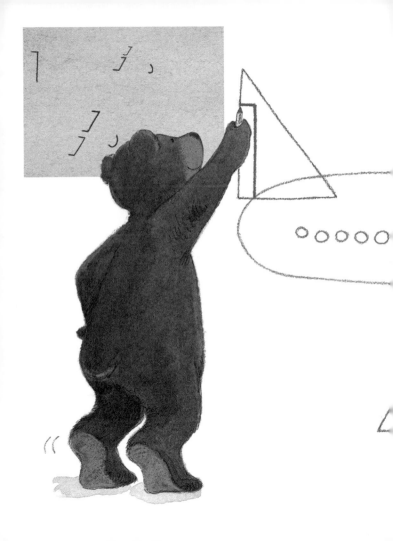

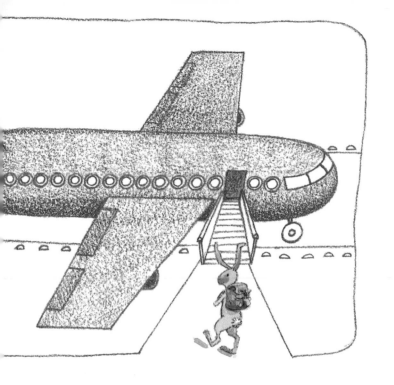

secrets of

PROSPERITY

J. DONALD WALTERS

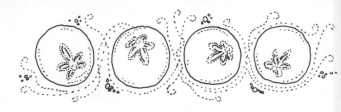

Hardbound edition, first printing 1993

Copyright 1993
J. Donald Walters

Text Illustrations: Karen White

Illustrations copyright 1993
Crystal Clarity, Publishers

ISBN 1-56589-037-X

10 9 8 7 6 5 4 3 2 1

PRINTED IN HONG KONG

Crystal ♀ *Clarity*
P U B L I S H E R S

14618 Tyler Foote Road, Nevada City, CA 95959
1 (800) 424-1055

A seed thought is offered for every day of the month. Begin a day at the appropriate date. Repeat the saying several times: first out loud, then softly, then in a whisper, and then only mentally. With each repetition, allow the words to become absorbed ever more deeply into your subconscious. Thus, gradually, you will acquire as complete an understanding as one might gain from a year's course in the subject. At this point, indeed, the truths set forth here will have become your own.

Keep the book open at the pertinent page throughout the day. Refer to it occasionally during moments of leisure. Relate the saying as often as possible to real situations in your life.

Then at night, before you go to bed, repeat the thought several times more. While falling asleep, carry the words into your subconscious, absorbing their positive influence into your whole being. Let it become thereby an integral part of your normal consciousness.

DAY ONE

the secret of

PROSPERITY

is . . . .

contentment, not a bank account.

DAY TWO

the secret of

ROSPERITY

is . . . .

happiness, for a determination
simply to be happy attracts
prosperity. Happiness is, at the same
time, the best definition
of prosperity.

DAY THREE

the secret of

PROSPERITY

is . . . .

generosity, for by sharing with
others the good that life gives us we
open up the well-springs
of abundance.

$\mathcal{D}$AY FOUR

the secret of

PROSPERITY

is . . . .

including the good of all in your own

quest for abundance.

Day Five

the secret of

ROSPERITY

is . . . .

recognition of the part you play in

the great Symphony of Life. For Life

will sustain you, if you attune

yourself to its harmonies.

DAY SIX

the secret of

PROSPERITY

is . . . .

working with, not against, life's

changing rhythms.

DAY SEVEN

the secret of

PROSPERITY

is . . . .

looking behind the obstacles you

face in life, to the opportunities

they represent.

DAY EIGHT

the secret of

PROSPERITY

is . . . .

seeing failure as a corrective,

not as a misfortune.

DAY NINE

the secret of

PROSPERITY

is . . . .

to diversify: not your financial
investments merely, as monetary
counselors recommend, but—more
importantly—your investments of
energy. Cultivate fresh ideas, fresh
interests, fresh relationships, fresh
reasons for enjoying your life.

DAY TEN

the secret of

PROSPERITY

is . . . .

faith—in yourself; in others;

in Life's abundance.

DAY ELEVEN

the secret of

PROSPERITY

is . . . .

to break the hypnosis of self-
limitation. The heights that any man
has attained can be attained again
by others—by anyone, each in his
own way—given enough time,
dedication, and focused energy.

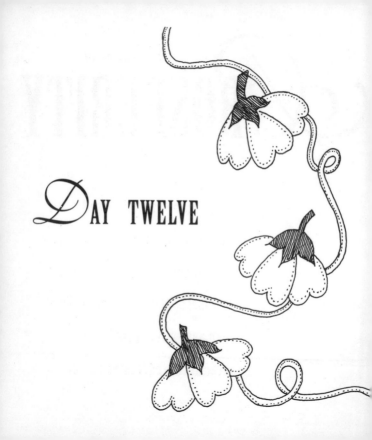

DAY TWELVE

the secret of

PROSPERITY

is . . . .

not to fritter energy away with trivial
desires. A leaky faucet, drop by drop,
wastes many gallons.

$\mathcal{D}$AY THIRTEEN

the secret of

PROSPERITY

is . . . .

finding pleasure in simplicity.

$\mathscr{D}$AY FOURTEEN

the secret of

PROSPERITY

is . . . .

holding positive expectations,

supported by a dynamic will.

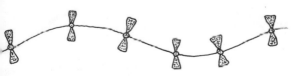

DAY FIFTEEN

the secret of

PROSPERITY

is . . . .

recognizing that people can be your

best investment. Be a true

friend to all.

$\mathcal{D}$AY SIXTEEN

the secret of

PROSPERITY

is . . . .

realizing that what you own is held
by you in trust. Treat it responsibly.
If you squander it, the trust will
pass to another.

DAY SEVENTEEN

the secret of

PROSPERITY

is . . . .

finding strength in yourself. Don't
wait for passing waves to propel
you forward.

Day eighteen

the secret of

PROSPERITY

is . . . .

realizing that one cannot truly
prosper by the diminishment of
others. Bless everyone. An expansion
of self-identity is a mark of
prosperity, and also a condition for
its attainment.

DAY NINETEEN

the secret of

PROSPERITY

is . . . .

extending a willing hand to the
needy; helping them, above all, to
help themselves.

DAY TWENTY

the secret of

PROSPERITY

is . . . .

common sense: Don't depend on luck,
but on a realistic assessment of
whatever situation you face. Only in
practical stages can you transform
"improbables" into realities.

DAY TWENTY-ONE

the secret of

PROSPERITY

is . . . .

to remember: The higher the
mountain, the harder the effort
needed to conquer it. Success is not
for the weak-hearted. It is for those
who never rest until they attain
their ideals.

DAY TWENTY-TWO

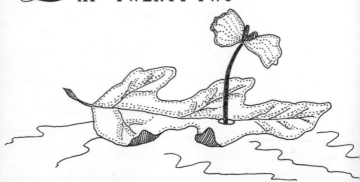

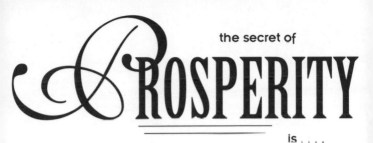

the secret of

PROSPERITY

is . . . .

the willingness to sacrifice

non-essentials for essentials.

Day TWENTY-THREE

the secret of

PROSPERITY

is . . . .

to live in the present: not in past

attainments, nor in future victories.

DAY TWENTY-FOUR

the secret of

PROSPERITY

is . . . .

the patience to adjust action to reality. In every setback, try to understand what life is trying to teach you.

Day TWENTY-FIVE

the secret of

PROSPERITY

is . . . .

envying no one. View others'
successes and failures
empathetically, as your own.

DAY TWENTY-SIX

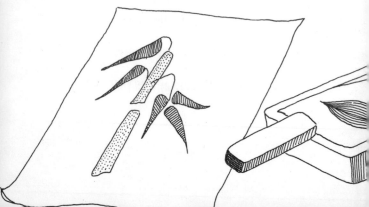

the secret of

PROSPERITY

is . . . .

inventiveness; success in any field
demands the creative outlook
of an artist.

DAY TWENTY-SEVEN

the secret of

PROSPERITY

is . . . .

to feed it daily with fresh, new
ideas—lest, like a still pond,
it stagnate.

DAY TWENTY-EIGHT

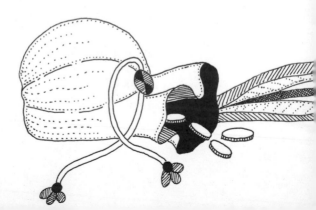

the secret of

PROSPERITY

is . . . .

to use it for the good of all, and not

to hoard it selfishly,

lest you stagnate.

DAY TWENTY-NINE

the secret of

PROSPERITY

is . . . .

a sense of proportion. Beware of

obsessions: They are an

ever-narrowing pathway.

DAY THIRTY

the secret of

PROSPERITY

is . . . .

to make time for singing. What, after
all, is prosperity, if in striving for it
one lose his capacity for song
and laughter?

DAY THIRTY-ONE

the secret of

PROSPERITY

is . . . .

remembering that the less importance you claim for yourself, the more importance you will acquire in the eyes of others. Their friendship will become, in time, your greatest asset.

Other Books in the **Secrets** Series
by J. Donald Walters

Design: Sara Cryer
Illustrations: Karen White
Typesetting: Robert Froelick
Photography: Frank Pedrick